The World of Work

Choosing a Career As a Firefighter

The job of a firefighter is very important—and very dangerous.

The World of Work

Choosing a Career As a Firefighter

Walter Oleksy

The Rosen Publishing Group, Inc.
New York

To Justin and Kaitlyn Ohde

Thanks to Fire Chief John Robberson and the firefighters of the Glenview, Illinois, Fire Department for their contributions to this book.

Published in 2000 by The Rosen Publishing Group, Inc.
29 East 21st Street, New York, NY 10010

First Edition 2000

Library of Congress Cataloging-in-Publication Data

Oleksy, Walter G., 1930–
   Choosing a career as a firefighter / Walter Oleksy.
    p.   cm.—(World of work)
   Includes bibliographical references and index.
   Summary: Outlines the educational requirements, qualifications, duties, salary, and employment outlook of firefighters.
   ISBN 0-8239-3245-1
   1. Fire extinction—Vocational guidance—Juvenile literature. 2. Fire fighters—Juvenile literature. [1. Fire extinction—Vocational guidance. 2. Fire fighters. 3. Fire extinction—Vocational guidance. 4. Vocational guidance.] I. Title. II. World of work (New York, N.Y.).
TH9119 .O43 2000
363.37'023—dc21   99-059417

Contents

Benjamin Franklin organized the first permanent fire company in
Philadelphia, Pennsylvania, in 1736.

Introduction

Welcome to the world of firefighting, one of the oldest, most important, and most exciting professions. If you are thinking of becoming a firefighter, you've taken the first step toward that goal by picking up this book. Here you will learn what a firefighter's work and life are like, and what it takes to become one.

Preventing and extinguishing fires is the main work of firefighters, and it dates back centuries. You could say that civilization began when prehistoric humans discovered fire. They learned that fire could provide light and warmth on a cold, dark night and that they could cook their food with it. They also learned that fire could be very destructive.

Over the centuries, bitter experience taught rulers the necessity of enforcing laws to prevent fires and of maintaining a professional force of firefighters. The

Roman emperor Augustus created the first official group of firefighters, who were all slaves, in 24 BC. The people in what is now France passed the first fire prevention law in 872 AD, requiring that all cooking and heating fires be put out by bedtime. In 1189, a law in London, England, required that all new buildings have stone walls and slate roofs instead of wooden ones.

In the American colonies, when New York was still in Dutch hands and known as New Amsterdam, a local law enacted in 1631 prohibited wooden chimneys. Fire inspections of buildings began in 1647. Colonial cities relied on volunteer firefighters who formed bucket brigades to put out fires. Benjamin Franklin organized the first permanent fire company in Philadelphia in 1736. New York City's first fire department opened the following year.

By the late 1800s, a series of devastating fires had claimed thousands of lives and destroyed whole sections of many American cities. These fires were mainly the result of poor building construction, inferior materials, and insufficient water supplies. Because most firemen worked at other jobs and only volunteered their services when a fire broke out, response times were slow. As a result, the late nineteenth century saw a trend away from volunteer firefighters toward full-time salaried professionals. By 1900, salaried fire departments with steam-propelled fire engines and telegraph fire-alarm systems, serviced by a wide network of fire hydrants, were common in the largest American cities.

Today nearly every community in the United States is served by an organized fire department. There are more than 30,000 fire departments in the nation. Of the approximately one million firefighters, some 280,000 are full-time career professionals, and nine out of ten of them work in municipal fire departments. Others are either "call" firefighters who are paid for each alarm they answer or volunteers who receive no pay.

The nation's 23,000 all-volunteer fire departments, mainly located in small towns and unincorporated rural areas, serve about a quarter of the U.S. population. The 1,800 all-professional departments serve about 44 percent of the population, mainly in the nation's cities. The remaining fire departments mix professional and volunteer staffs. Some firefighters work on federal installations such as army or navy bases. Others work at airports and in large manufacturing plants. Firefighters are everywhere.

More than 1.4 million fires occur each year in the United States. They cause about 6,000 deaths, hundreds of thousands of injuries, and billions of dollars in property damage annually. More fire-related deaths occur in the United States than in any other industrialized nation. About 100,000 fires in the United States are deliberately set. This is more than in any other country in the world. Arson causes about 1,000 deaths a year in the United States and is responsible for over $1.5 billion in fire-related damage.

To become a firefighter, you must be in excellent physical condition. Your work will often be very strenuous as well as dangerous. The qualification process for firefighters is highly competitive. A college degree in fire science can be very helpful, as can experience as a volunteer firefighter. You must pass a comprehensive physical

Early fire trucks ran on steam-propelled engines.

examination and you must prepare for and pass an extensive written examination before you can become a firefighter.

Exciting but Dangerous Work

Firefighting can be exciting, but it is also an extremely hazardous occupation. Flames, smoke, toxic fumes, and collapsing buildings create danger. Over one hundred firefighters die and more than 100,000 are injured fighting fires in the United States each year.

Your salary and benefits will be good, but many people choose firefighting as a career because it's a very personally rewarding occupation. Saving lives and protecting property from fire is a very noble kind of work that brings great personal satisfaction. Firefighters feel that their work is important and that it matters to society. They are right.

As a firefighter, you will also develop a strong sense of comradeship with your fellow firefighters, because battling a fire is not done alone. It is a team effort. The job requires cooperation and alertness from every member of the team. You'll share the dangers the way that soldiers do in a war. Firefighters often feel like brothers and sisters as they work together to put out or prevent fires.

In the following pages, you'll learn more about the career of firefighting. You'll learn what the work is like, what clothing and equipment are required, what kind of training is necessary, and what the various kinds of jobs performed by firefighters are. Then you can ask yourself if a career as a firefighter is for you.

Duties of a Firefighter 1

If you become a firefighter, you'll have a variety of duties to perform both at the firehouse and while out fighting a fire. You'll have to be able to respond to fire and medical emergencies, use hoses and ladders, perform acts of rescue or give artificial respiration, and know how to extinguish various types of fires.

Your duties will also involve cleaning equipment and attending training sessions and fire drills. You may also be assigned to inspect buildings to ensure the enforcement of fire regulations or to handle radio and telephone communications. And yes, you may learn to drive fire trucks or rescue and ambulance vehicles.

Your work schedule will depend on the policy at the fire station you are assigned to. In many cities, you may be on duty for twenty-four hours, then off for forty-eight hours, with an extra day off at intervals. In other cities, you may work a day shift of ten hours for three or four days, or a night shift of fourteen hours for three or four nights. You may then get three or four days off before repeating the schedule. If you work in a large city in the heavily populated eastern states, you may work a regular forty-hour week or up to fifty-six hours a week. When fighting a fire, however, you may also work extra hours until the blaze is put under control or out.

Living twenty-four hours a day at a fire station may not be for everyone, especially married men and women and those with children. It takes some adjusting to such a life, but many say they like it.

At the Fire Station

While on duty as a firefighter, you'll eat and sleep at the fire house. It will become like a second home for you. You will also take turns shopping for groceries, preparing meals, and cleaning up afterward.

Between fire calls, your duties at the station include keeping the station clean as well as cleaning and maintaining the equipment you use. You will also have classroom training so you can learn how to use the latest equipment or practice techniques in firefighting. In addition, you

For firefighters, the fire house is like a second home because it is where they eat and sleep.

will take part in practice fire drills that test your firefighting knowledge, your alertness, and your ability to respond quickly.

When you are not cleaning, polishing, or performing some other duty at the fire station, you can relax. You can read, study, watch television, or pursue other personal activities. Most fire stations have exercise equipment in recreation rooms. You'll be able to get free use of the equipment to maintain your physical fitness.

You will also probably do fire-prevention work, inspecting schools and other public buildings for conditions that may cause a fire. You will look to see if flammable materials are safely stored and whether fire extinguishers are present and operable. You will check on the number and working condition of fire escapes and fire doors. You will also visit schools and civic organizations to educate the public about fire prevention and fire safety measures.

At a Fire

When you are on duty at the fire station, you'll have to stop whatever you're doing and respond rapidly when an alarm sounds. You'll learn how to be out of the station in response to a fire call within twenty seconds of the alarm going off, no matter what time of day or night and regardless of weather. Sometimes you'll spend long hours fighting fires in heavy rain or snowstorms and in extremely cold or hot weather.

At fires, you'll perform specific duties assigned by your company captain, lieutenant, or another fire department officer. The officer, usually called a fire chief, tells the engine company firefighters which hoses to deploy and how much water pressure to use. After the hoses are attached to hydrants and the pumps are started, the

A firefighter's task may be to hook up hoses to a hydrant at a fire.

firefighters direct water onto the flames. The officer stays in communication with the station's dispatcher by walkie-talkie radio, asking for more help if needed.

Your duties at a fire may involve connecting hoses to fire hydrants, operating a fire pump, or placing ladders. Your duties may change several times during a fire, so you'll be expected to know many different firefighting activities. These varied duties include operating fire apparatus and driving emergency rescue ambulances or other vehicles. Some departments operate fireboats when fighting fires on waterways or along shores.

If you're a ladder company firefighter, you'll search for people or animals trapped in a burning building. You may have to smash windows, break doors open, or cut holes in the roof with axes and saws to allow smoke, toxic gases, and heat to escape. After a rescue, you may have to administer first aid. This may require attending to cuts and bruises, providing oxygen for smoke inhalation victims, performing artificial respiration, or stabilizing a heart attack victim.

The potential for danger is always present at a fire. You may risk injury or even death if you're trapped in a burning building. Floors may suddenly give way under you or walls may fall on you or block your exit. Inhaling too much smoke is often as dangerous as being burned. Also, you may come in contact with poisonous or explosive gases and chemicals.

After a fire, you'll work in cleanup operations. You'll make certain that no live embers remain that could restart the fire. This may involve tearing down walls and ceilings or prying up floors. Afterward you and your comrades will sweep and mop up areas not burned and clean up the debris.

A fireboat puts out fires on the water.

When you return to your station, you'll have to clean your dirty equipment. Hoses must be stretched out and washed, then hung to dry on the hose tower. Later the hoses are rolled up for storage. If you wore a mask and used an air tank at the fire, the mask must be cleaned and the tank refilled with oxygen. When you have finished those chores, you have to clean and put away your tools. You have to be ready for the next fire call as fast as possible.

Crews, Companies, and Battalions

Most firefighters are assigned to crews (teams of firefighters) called companies. A company usually has an officer, such as a fire chief, and an apparatus operator. It also has one or two firefighters who are assigned to a specific piece of fire equipment. The crew may be called an engine or pumper company, or a ladder or truck company. In large cities, one or two fire companies may be assigned to each fire station.

The hours you work as a firefighter are called a shift. The members of each shift are called a platoon. They may be called platoon A, B, or C. At larger fire departments with more than five or six fire stations, a platoon is broken down into battalions. These are groups of fire companies that protect specific parts of a city.

How to Become a Firefighter

2

If you become a firefighter in the United States or Canada, you'll probably work for the fire protection services of a local government such as a city or town. Visit your local fire department to learn about job opportunities as a firefighter.

Education

In most local or regional fire departments, you will have to have at least a high school diploma before you can apply to become a firefighter. Many colleges offer degrees in fire science. You can prepare to take an examination for firefighting in the city or town where you'd like to work.

In some fire departments, you may get pre-entry training. This tests your ability to carry heavy firefighting equipment and will determine whether or not you are afraid of heights or of being in small places, such as crawl spaces. Pre-entry training also tests your ability to work together with others.

It is very important to have an education in both math and English. These subjects will be required to understand some technical aspects of firefighting such as fire chemistry, fluid hydraulics, electricity, and building construction.

Probationary Periods

If you are a new firefighter, you will serve a probationary period of about a year. In some fire departments, the period may be as short as six months or as long as eighteen months. During this period, you will take part in extensive training to see if you have the ability to perform the strenuous work of a firefighter. You'll also undergo more classroom and field training. To complete the probationary period, you must spend time on the job and pass a series of examinations. When you pass the probationary period, you are officially a firefighter.

Promotions

If you want to continue in the "combat arm" of fire service, there are several opportunities for advancement. The next level above basic firefighter is that of

Hazardous material technicians are specialized firefighters.

apparatus operator—meaning you'll drive one of the fire trucks. From that position you can advance to become a company commander, then a chief officer.

If you want to advance instead into one of the specialized fields of firefighting, there are several opportunities. You could become an emergency medical technician (EMT), a hazardous material technician (HMT), or a paramedic, aircraft crash rescuer, harbor or waterfront firefighter, fire inspector, training officer, or arson investigator. Each of these specialized jobs involves more schooling and experience.

A Firefighter's Day

3

When you work as a firefighter, few days are ever alike. You may spend the whole day cleaning and polishing, which can be boring. You may be called to a fire that turns out to be a false alarm. Or you may fight a huge blaze in a home, a high-rise office, a hospital, or some other public building. No matter how quiet or busy your day may be, you'll have to be prepared for any emergency.

Traffic Rescue

While you're with your platoon having lunch in the station, a call comes in for a response to a traffic collision—a "cut and rescue." You all hurry into your fire-fighting clothes—flame-retardant pants, boots, turnout coat, and helmet—and respond to a Code Three. En route to the crash scene, the fire truck you are on flashes its red light and blares its siren. One or two other engine companies may also respond to the call.

When you arrive at the crash scene, you learn that a motorist is trapped behind the steering wheel of one of the two cars involved. A passenger in the other car is already being treated by paramedics.

If you're a member of a truck crew, you'll unload a hydraulic rescue tool while other firefighters lay hose lines. They'll be ready in case spilled gasoline catches fire or one or both of the cars explode into flames. You may have to cut the motorist's seat belt to get him out, using a hydraulic tool called the "Jaws of Life."

Paramedics give medical aid to the motorist while maintaining radio contact with the emergency room of the nearest hospital. Soon the motorist is in an ambulance speeding to the hospital, thanks to your brave work and that of your fellow firefighters.

A False Alarm

You may be asleep at 2 AM on your twenty-four-hour shift when the alarm bell shocks you and your comrades awake. As you hurry into your fire clothes, you hear the dispatcher call out the address of the fire.

Firefighters getting ready at the fire house to respond to a call that has just come in.

Maybe the fire is in a drugstore in a shopping mall half a mile away from the fire station. You know the mall and drugstore well from being there on inspection tours. En route to the fire, you recall as much as you can about the drugstore building. You know that it is a one-story brick-and-wood structure containing many flammables that could explode. This could be a very dangerous fire call.

When you arrive at the mall, you learn that there isn't a fire there after all. A cat accidentally set off the drugstore's fire alarm. On the way back to the station, you figure you were lucky. It could have been a very big and explosive fire.

Public Assistance Call

There may be occasions when the task you are called upon to perform will not seem very dramatic, but to the people involved you will have made all the difference. A senior citizen may accidentally lock himself in the bathroom while home with his wife. She telephones for help, and you arrive in a Code Two response. Since it is not a life-threatening emergency, the driver doesn't sound the fire truck's siren or flash its red lights. In a short time, you have pried open the lock and rescued the man.

As a firefighter, you will respond to an average of five calls a shift. However, if you work in a large city, the number of calls could be greater. In fact, you may be called to one emergency after another every hour that you're on duty. You will learn to always expect the unexpected.

Equipment and Fire Trucks

4

Firefighters have very specialized vehicles and equipment. This equipment is designed and constructed with the latest advances in technology in mind.

Ladders

Ladders are among the most essential and frequently used pieces of equipment that a firefighter has. They were first carried on fire engines in the eighteenth century so that firefighters could rescue people trapped on the upper floors of burning buildings.

The average fire ladder can reach a height of 100 feet (30 meters), although a few can extend as far as about 164 feet (50 meters). They are usually mounted on turntable-like disks on the fire truck so that firefighters have great flexibility in pointing the ladder in any direction. Hoses are often run up the ladder to nozzles mounted at the top, so that firefighters can more accurately direct streams of water.

You will also use elevating platforms and aerial towers. In one type, the platform is mounted on a jointed boom that travels in an arc. In another, the platform is mounted on an extendable or telescopic boom like an aerial ladder. Aerial towers can reach up to one hundred feet. Beyond that, a truck-mounted hydraulic platform ladder with a "bucket" at the far end can carry you up to the seventh or eighth story of a burning building.

Fire Extinguishers

Another very important firefighting tool is the portable fire extinguisher. You'll use it to put out small fires in their early stages, such as a fire that flashes up on the kitchen stove or in the oven, and also to fight more explosive fires.

Modern multipurpose dry-chemical fire extinguishers that can be used to put out a wide range of fires were introduced in the early 1960s. The type of chemical in the extinguisher depends upon the kinds of fires it was designed to smother, and these different types of fires have been classified by the National Fire Protection Agency.

Class A Fires
Class A fires involve ordinary combustibles such as paper, wood, and cloth. You can extinguish them by using water-based liquids or by smothering the fires with certain dry chemicals.

Class B Fires
These types of fires involve flammable and combustible liquids, greases, and similar volatile materials. You can put them out by depriving the fire of air, preventing the release of combustible vapors, or by interrupting the combustion process. Class B fire extinguishers usually contain dry chemicals, carbon dioxide, foam, or a liquefied gas known as halon.

Class C Fires
Class C fires are those involving electrical equipment. You will put them out with an agent that is electrically nonconducting, to avoid getting a shock. Dry chemicals, carbon dioxide, and halon extinguishers are used to fight these fires.

Class D Fires
These types of fires are caused by the burning of combustible metals such as

magnesium. Fighting them requires a smothering and heat-absorbing agent that does not react with the burning metals.

Other Equipment

As a firefighter, you will also have to become familiar with radio communications equipment and with electric lights and generators for fighting night fires. You will learn to work portable pumps and equipment that generates foam for smothering fires burning in flammable liquids. You will learn to handle various types of axes, pikes, and crowbars so that you can get into burning buildings quickly.

Fire Vehicles

In 1679 the city of Boston imported the first fire engine to be used in America. The first fire engine made in America was designed and built by Thomas Lote of New York in 1743. Today there are a great variety of specialized vehicles at most fire stations. Some fire trucks weigh more than seventy tons.

The pumper is a water tender with an engine and pumps. It carries about 500 gallons (1,900 liters) of water—enough for

Ladder trucks allow firefighters to reach the upper floors or roof of
a burning building.

you and your fellow firefighters to put out a small fire. The pumper also carries hoses that firefighters attach to fire hydrants to pump water onto a fire from a city's main underground water supply. Extension ladders are carried on the roof of the pumper.

Ladder trucks carry ladders and hoses. Some ladder trucks are equipped with hydraulic ladders that can carry firefighters to the upper floors or roof of a burning building. Aerial ladder trucks have metal ladders that rest on the back of the truck and extend to two or three times their stored length. They enable firefighters to reach fires high up in buildings. They have a long arm called a boom with a platform, called a bucket, on which the firefighter stands. Hydraulic booms can send aerial ladders as high as 203 feet (62 meters).

Special rescue trucks have large lockers that contain rakes, shovels, emergency lights, maps, tools, stretchers, and breathing equipment. They may also hold cutting equipment that is used to slice through metal cars in which victims may be trapped.

Salaries, Benefits, and Advancement

5

You can earn more money in other careers, but they may not be as secure or rewarding as being a firefighter. In many other jobs, you can get laid off during hard times or if your employer sells or goes out of business. While you won't get rich being a firefighter, the pay is fairly good. And it is unlikely that you will lose your job, because firefighting is one of the most stable occupations.

Salaries differ from one fire department to another, since they are regulated by local governments. Your average starting salary as a full-time firefighter will be about $20,000 a year. After five or more years, you can earn about $30,000. Salaries are higher in cities, especially the largest cities and those in the western states. There you can earn up to $40,000 or $50,000.

Some fire departments also add "longevity pay" to salaries. This is extra money paid in recognition of competent work, even if the firefighter has not been promoted for up to ten years. The extra pay may be about $1,000 a year. Bonuses may also be given if you have received advanced education in the field of fire protection. As a firefighter, you may be promoted once or twice before you retire. If you reach the top job of a chief fire officer, you may earn about $80,000 a year.

Benefits

Benefits can add the equivalent of another 50 percent to your firefighter's salary. They may include the following:

Insurance

Firefighters pay less for life and medical insurance than do people in other professions, and it usually covers the immediate family. If injured while on duty, firefighters are covered by their department's disability insurance or retirement plan. If a firefighter is forced to retire early because of a job-related injury, he or she may receive benefits equal to his or her income before becoming disabled.

Physical Fitness

Many fire departments provide free exercise equipment in station gyms so that firefighters can keep themselves in top physical condition. If you are the kind of person who is likely to spend money on membership in a health club, this could be a significant benefit.

Allowances

Firefighters usually get a clothing allowance of $20 to $30 a month to keep uniforms clean and serviceable. Most of the fireproof protective clothing worn is provided and replaced by the fire department.

Education

You will probably be encouraged to receive education beyond a high school or college degree. You will be reimbursed for tuition and books. The education, however, may have to relate to some aspect of firefighting.

Sick Leave and Vacation

Like most other public employees, you'll be paid for a certain number of days off because of sickness. You'll also get at least two weeks of paid vacation a year.

Pride

One of the biggest benefits of being a firefighter is intangible and cannot be

Firefighters are proud that they care about one other and about the safety of people and animals everywhere.

measured in terms of money. It is the feeling of camaraderie among firefighters that extends not only to your own battalion but to firefighters everywhere in the world. You become part of a fraternity of men and women who care about each other and the safety of people and animals everywhere. No amount of money can compare to the feeling of satisfaction you'll get as a firefighter, especially after you have helped to save a life during a fire.

Meet Some Firefighters 6

Paul Klicker, thirty-three years old, has spent six years as a firefighter-paramedic for the Glenview, Illinois, Fire Department in the northwest suburbs of Chicago. The village's population is about 40,000, but its fire department also serves the nearby smaller village of Golf and the surrounding unincorporated areas, which brings the total population served to about 58,000.

Klicker works out of one of the village's three fire stations, which have a combined total of eighty-two firefighters and supervisory and support personnel. The firefighters respond to about 6,500 calls a year, about half of them alarms that may be a fire. The other calls are for emergency medical services, everything from auto accidents to heart attacks to kitchen stove burns.

"After working as a golf course manager, I tested for a firefighter and was accepted by Glenview," Klicker says. "I served a two-year probationary period during which I attended a Fire Academy to learn firefighting skills and how to operate firefighting tools. I also completed paramedic training and Emergency Medical Technician School."

Just as Klicker finished talking about his background, a Code Three fire alarm sounded and he rushed to an ambulance to join others responding to the call. An automatic fire alarm had gone off at a nearby elementary school.

Klicker returned in about fifteen minutes. "It was a false alarm," he reported. "Someone or something accidentally set off the alarm." Nonetheless, two engine companies, a fire truck, an ambulance, and a command officer had responded. Klicker simply reset the alarm so that it would be operational in a real emergency.

"That was okay," says Klicker. "I'd rather go to one false alarm than a hundred fires, because with real fires lives and property are in danger."

When asked about the most exciting call he's been on, Klicker replied, "It was when a young man about twenty-one years old called 911 to say that he was having an asthma attack, and then fell unconscious. The call was traced to his home, and when we got there, since the doors were locked, we had to force entry.

"We found him in cardiac arrest. He wasn't breathing and he had no pulse. Death would occur in four to six minutes. I gave him emergency aid, including adrenaline to stimulate his heart. Then we rushed him to the hospital by ambulance. It was on a Friday and he remained there over the weekend. But he was well enough on Monday to come to the fire station and thank us for saving his life."

Glenview's fire chief, John Robberson, adds, "That young man could have been buried on Monday, if it hadn't been for Paul and his training as a paramedic."

"It was a very rewarding feeling to know that I helped save a life," Klicker says. "Something like that is what I call a silent paycheck. You can't put the feeling of saving a life into a paycheck."

A husband and a father, Klicker says there are other rewards to his occupation. "There's a real bond between firefighters.

It's like having a second family. And my three-year-old son loves the fire trucks."

Klicker has some advice for young people thinking of a career as a firefighter. "Take science and math courses, physiology and anatomy classes, and take physical fitness seriously. And take part in team activities, such as sports or working on the school newspaper. Firefighting is a team effort that plays out on every call. One person doesn't do everything. We depend on each other. Like I said, firefighters are like a family. It's a great job."

Chief Robberson agrees. He began as a volunteer with the Glenview Fire Department in 1973 after graduating from DePaul University in Chicago with a degree in business administration. Over the next eleven years, he worked his way up from firefighter-paramedic to director of emergency medical training, and then became chief when his predecessor retired in 1984.

Asked what he looks for in a firefighter candidate, Robberson says, "Firefighters have to be service-oriented. They have to want to help others and be willing to risk their lives doing it. Because promotions are limited, they have to be satisfied in their work. As Paul says, it is a great job, whether in 'combat' as he is, fighting fires, or being part of the administrative team that keeps a fire department the best it can be."

Tom Detloff, a twenty-five-year veteran with the Glenview Fire Department, says, "I've never felt my life to be in danger fighting a fire because of the training and teamwork." For Detloff, the hardest part about being a firefighter is responding to auto accidents. "You try not to hurt people, removing them from a car wreck, but sometimes it just can't be helped, in order to save their life. And believe me, we feel their pain, too."

Female Firefighters

Tracy Albarino, eighteen, works as a volunteer firefighter while attending John Jay College of Criminal Justice in New York City. "I'm the first and only female in the Manhattan fire station I'm assigned to," says Albarino. "I like the work because it's pretty exciting and satisfying.

"I come from a long line of firefighters, so I have a strong desire to be one. But I'm also interested in the legal aspects of

More women become firefighters every year.

arson, so I'm double majoring in criminal justice and fire science, with a concentration in fire investigation."

Eva Fitts, thirty-one, tells how and why she became a firefighter in California. "I was hired by the Rialto Fire Department. My dad is a captain in the neighboring city of San Bernardino, where he has been a firefighter for thirty-five years.

"I became a firefighter because I wanted to be like my dad, who is and always will be my hero. My parents discouraged my interest in the fire service until my dad supervised a new recruit named Debbie.

She did such a good job, it changed his mind about women being firefighters.

"Then, with my parents' encouragement and blessing, I began testing in 1989 and was hired two years later. I love my job and my department!"

Vicki Davis, twenty-six, joined the Amelia Fire Department on the east side of Cincinnati, Ohio, as an emergency medical technician in 1997. "Then I started helping at the fires and passed the tests to become a certified firefighter there.

"I first thought of becoming a firefighter when I was a kid, watching and chasing after fire trucks that drove down the street. I always thought to myself, 'I'd love to do that.'

"One day, my older brother and I talked about my becoming a firefighter. It was always a dream, then one day it happened. I joined our local fire department as a volunteer. Now I plan to make it my career.

"I've gained a lot of respect for firefighters. I enjoy everything that goes along with the job. Even having to roll hose. This is not a field for everyone, but it is something anyone can try."

How to Prepare for a Career as a Firefighter

7

There was a time when all it took to become a firefighter was to be strong and brave. But modern firefighting technology has changed things. Today, in addition to strength and courage, you must have quite a bit of education and training.

You may be able to pass the physical tests to become a firefighter by being in good physical condition. You may also be able to pass the entrance examination with just a high school diploma. But some fire departments require candidates to have taken at least some college courses, especially those related to the duties of firefighting. You may be able to take introductory or basic fire science courses at your local community college.

Most fire departments require that firefighters be at least twenty-one years old. In order to be in the best possible condition to pass a physical examination that will test your strength and endurance, it is important that you don't smoke or use drugs. Smoking has been linked to breathing disorders and heart and circulatory diseases. Smoking reduces the power of your lungs to distribute oxygen to your body. Because less oxygen goes to the muscles, you can't run or climb as fast or carry as much as a nonsmoker.

Drugs alter mental functions. Drug testing is part of the screening process for firefighters. If you test positive for drug use, you won't be hired. Moderate consumption of alcohol or caffeine is acceptable, but excessive consumption can be harmful.

It is equally important not to be excessively overweight or underweight. Being too heavy requires the muscles, heart, and lungs to work harder, especially when performing strenuous tasks. Being too thin may prevent a person from carrying heavy equipment, and that person may tire more easily.

Basic skills in reading, writing, and mathematics are essential in preparing to be a firefighter. If you take classes in science, building construction, and auto mechanics, so much the better. Since both physical fitness and teamwork are very important in firefighting, taking part in competitive sports in high school is also beneficial.

Any summer or part-time work that lets you use your hands and requires some physical effort also helps. You might work outdoors with a landscaping crew, or help build decks or houses for a construction company. You might pump gas, change tires, or repair cars at a local gas station. These and other physically demanding jobs that also require some thinking will help you to gain the right kind of experience. They will show others that you can do physically and mentally challenging jobs, be part of a team, and work under supervision.

Pre-Employment Training

Some fire departments offer high school students pre-employment training. One such program is the Fire Explorer program, organized in cooperation with the Boy Scouts of America. Open to both boys and girls of high school age, it offers minimal training in controlling fires, preventing fires, rescuing victims, and performing emergency medical procedures. Scouts may even go to fires with fire companies to observe them in action. A similar opportunity is offered in

Firefighters must be extremely strong—able to lift heavy equipment as well as people from burning buildings.

some parts of the nation by Regional Occupational Programs. This group provides career training in fire protection.

Many colleges offer courses leading to a degree in fire science. Such a degree can be one of the best qualifications you can have when applying for a position as a firefighter.

Most fire departments have recruit training programs, in which you will learn what the firefighting duties are and how to perform them. After six to eight weeks of training, you will have to take both physical and written tests.

One of the best ways to prepare for a career as a firefighter is to study a typical examination that candidates must pass. For an example, take a look at the New York City exam in a manual called *Firefighter*, an Arco book published by Macmillan.

Firefighter Examinations

If you want to become a firefighter, first you have to pass both a physical and written test.

The physical test will involve a physical examination as well as activities that test muscular strength and endurance and body flexibility. Fully suited in firefighter's clothing, you may be required to walk on a motorized stepmill at the rate of fifty-nine steps per minute for five minutes, carrying a weighted vest, oxygen tank, and gloves.

Another test may require you to be similarly dressed and lift a twenty-foot aluminum ladder, place it against a wall, and then raise a twenty-four-foot extension ladder, all in less than sixteen seconds. Other physical tests involve carrying heavy hoses, climbing a rope, and bashing a twelve-pound sledgehammer against a rubber pad that measures the force of the blow. In a search test, you'll crawl through a winding, eighty-foot-long dark tunnel only three feet high, wearing heavy clothing and carrying firefighter gear. You will have to complete the crawl in less than ninety-six seconds.

The written examination tests your knowledge of firefighting and your ability to reason and make judgments. It also tests your basic knowledge of mechanics by asking questions such as: What does a carburetor do? How does water pressure work? How does electric current flow?

Women Firefighters

If you are female and want to become a firefighter, the career is open to you, although meeting the physical requirements may not be easy. You'll have to compete with men on equal terms in passing physical tests that measure strength and endurance.

About 5,000 women are full-time firefighters and officers in the United States. Several hundred hold the rank of lieutenant or captain, and about forty are district chiefs, battalion chiefs, division chiefs, or assistant chiefs. More women become career firefighters every year. About another 40,000 women in the United States are volunteer firefighters. Their numbers are also increasing each year.

The first woman to become a career firefighter in the United States was Judith Livers, the wife of a firefighter. In 1974 she was hired by the Arlington County, Virginia, Fire Department, where she now holds the rank of battalion chief. The first known volunteer woman firefighter was Molly Williams. An African-American and a former slave, she worked in a New York City fire station in 1818.

Obstacles Women Firefighters Face

Aside from meeting the physical requirements, women face other special challenges. According to Women in the Fire Service, Inc., a nonprofit organization, these include:

1. Resistance from some male firefighters who may be skeptical about women's competence as firefighters.
2. Male firefighters' emotional attachment to an otherwise all-male workplace.
3. Male firefighters' uncertainty about how to act when working with women, and vice versa.

Furthermore, women firefighters may not find a fire station's physical facilities adequate for them. Since fire stations are built to accommodate men, women may be concerned about their sleeping, bathing, restroom, and clothes-changing facilities.

Women firefighters need alternative protective gear and uniforms that are not designed for men. Women also need special leave policies if they become pregnant. After children are born, women need special child-care options if they work twenty-four-hour shifts.

Apart from these concerns, women face the same problems as male firefighters. The work is physically demanding and often dangerous. There is a high level of stress caused by exposure to trauma and tragedy. Work schedules require nights and weekends away from home and family. Both male and female firefighters must accept that they will sleep irregular hours or get too little sleep because of their work schedules.

But, as for men, the rewards for female firefighters can be just as great, namely, the satisfaction of performing work that can save lives and property. For more information on women firefighters, see the For More Information section at the back of this book.

Other Firefighting Careers 8

There are opportunities to work as a firefighter in places other than city or town fire departments, and some of these special positions are unique and exciting.

Private Fire Departments

Many large companies that deal with chemicals have their own private fire departments, though some may be small and only staff one or two firefighters. Private airports and companies in the aerospace industry such as Boeing and McDonnell Douglas also have their own fire departments. These jobs often concentrate more on fire prevention than actual firefighting.

Forest Firefighters

If you like the outdoors, you may consider becoming a firefighter in a state or national forest or park. The three largest federal

Forest firefighting is extremely dangerous. Special airplanes are used to help firefighters combat forest fires.

agencies that hire firefighters are the U.S. Forest Service, the National Park Service, and the Bureau of Land Management.

If you become a firefighter who works in a state or national forest or park, you will be specially trained to fight forest fires. Forest firefighting is a very dangerous occupation, and many men and women have lost their lives in forest blazes.

Forest firefighters often put fires out by creating a "fire line." Using chain saws and hand tools and fire itself, they clear a wide strip of land of everything that can burn, thereby preventing the fire from spreading across it. Forest firefighters are often aided by pilots who fly their planes over a fire and drop fire-retarding chemicals onto the blaze. Helicopter crews may also dump thousands of gallons of water on a forest fire. The water is poured over the fire from a large bucket.

Forest firefighters, who sometimes have to hike several miles to the site of a fire, are called smoke chasers. Besides wearing fire-retarding clothing and helmets, they carry a backpack containing an ax, a shovel, and other equipment weighing about one hundred pounds. They are often aided by smoke jumpers. Smoke jumpers are firefighters who parachute from an airplane to help the ground crews put out forest fires. The first smoke jumpers were stunt men or women who performed at air shows, walking on the wings of planes. Today, smoke jumpers are highly trained in the specialized work of fighting forest fires. They have to be in excellent physical condition and may work twenty-four hours straight, or even more. About 400 smoke jumpers, fifteen of them women, work out of eleven bases in the western states.

Firefighters on Boats

The U.S. Navy and the Coast Guard are two of the biggest employers of firefighters who work on fireboats. Many fire departments of coastal cities and those on lakes and rivers also have fireboats manned by firefighters. The boats are specially equipped to pump thousands of gallons of water onto a fire that breaks out on another boat or along the shore in a waterfront building.

Fire Prevention Careers

Several types of companies hire men and women to fill jobs in fire prevention. Among these are fire alarm companies, fire extinguisher companies, and fire sprinkler companies. While the work does not involve fighting fires, installing, maintaining, and repairing fire prevention equipment can also be a rewarding career.

A field related to fire service is that of fire protection engineer. Jobs are plentiful for those who can design fire safety and fire prevention programs for a wide range of industries, cities and towns, government agencies, the military, and schools. The work often requires a lot of technical knowledge and computer skills.

The Future for Firefighters

As the nation's population grows and the need for fire protection increases, more firefighters will be needed in the years ahead. While the number of city fire departments and firefighting personnel is expected to increase, even more growth is expected in the suburbs of major cities and smaller rural communities. Most firefighters remain in their jobs until they retire, but then departments need to replace them with new firefighters.

As in most industries, the future of firefighting will involve the use of more technical and computerized aids. To keep up with developments in the industry, you will spend more time learning and being tested on the technology. Firefighting equipment is expected to get smaller and lighter in weight, as well as more efficient in putting out fires of all kinds. Fighting fires in the future may involve more technical than physical abilities, since the increasing use of hazardous materials in business and industry creates more dangerous fires.

As a twenty-first century firefighter, you'll have to learn how to use new chemicals and water additives to fight industrial fires. Knowledge of these substances may become as important to you as your safety coat and gloves, or your department's ladder and hose.

Ask Yourself

One of the best ways to decide whether or not a career as a firefighter is for you is to ask yourself some personal questions. If you have completed high school, these include:

1. Am I physically fit?
2. Am I afraid of heights?
3. Am I afraid of enclosed areas?
4. Can I take orders from superiors?
5. Can I work well with others?
6. Could I risk my life to save others?
7. Am I willing to keep learning and training?

Glossary

aerial ladder A long metal extension ladder mounted on a fire truck.

arson The act of deliberately setting a fire.

"call" firefighters Unsalaried firefighters who are paid for each alarm they answer, or volunteers who get no pay.

crawl spaces Low-ceilinged places in basements or attics.

"cut and rescue" An emergency call, usually involving an auto crash.

dispatcher A fire station's telephone operator.

engine company The branch of a fire company whose job is to stretch out the hose lines and put out a fire.

extinguish To put out a fire.

extinguisher A pressurized container filled with water or chemicals used to put out fires.

false alarm A call to a fire that turns out not to be a fire.

flammable Capable of burning or prone to catch fire.

hazardous Very dangerous.

inhalation The act of breathing in, as in breathing in smoke.

ladder company or truck company The branch of a fire company whose job is to raise ladders, rescue victims, and ventilate a building that is on fire.

paramedic A firefighter trained in providing emergency medical services.

platoon The members of a shift.

probationary period The first months or year that a firefighter is on the job.

pumper A truck with engine-driven pumps that take water from a curb-side hydrant.

rookie A beginning firefighter.

shift The hours a firefighter is on duty.

ventilation Term used for opening the roofs, doors, windows, and other openings in a building so toxic gases and smoke can escape.

For More Information

Check with your local fire department for information on careers in firefighting, or contact the following agencies.

In the United States

International Association of Fire Chiefs
1329 18th Street NW
Washington, DC 20036

International Association of Fire Fighters
1750 New York Avenue NW
Washington, DC 20036

National Fire Protection Association
Batterymarch Park
Quincy, MA 02269

Women in the Fire Service, Inc.
P.O. Box 5446
Madison, WI 53705
Web site: http://www.wfsi.org.

In Canada

Canadian Association of Fire Fighters
11J Rayborn Crescent
St. Albert, Alberta T8N 5C3

For Further Reading

Books

Andriuolo, Robert. *Everything You Need to Know to Score High on Firefighter.* New York: Macmillan, 1997.

Coleman, Ronny J. *Opportunities in Fire Protection Services.* Lincolnwood, IL: VGM Career Horizons, 1997.

Delsohn, Steve. *The Fire Inside.* New York: HarperCollins, 1996.

Magazines

American Firefighters
Suite 61
Cheney, WA 99004

Firehouse Magazine
Cygnus Publishing Co.
445 Broad Hollow Road, Suite 21
Melville, NY 11747

Index

About the Author

Walter Oleksy is a freelance writer and the author of over forty books for adults and young people. He lives in Glenview, Illinois, with his dog, Max, a black Lab mix who loves to talk and take walks.

Photo Credits

p.6 © Archive Photos; pp. 2, 32, 43, 48 © Pictor; p. 11 © FPG; pp. 15, 17 © Ron Rovtar; pp. 19, 23, 54 © Superstock; pp. 26, 37 by Thaddeus Harden.

Design and Layout

Michael J. Caroleo